PIANO PLAY-ALONG

AUDIO ACCESS INCLUDED

TODAY'S HITS

CONTENTS

To access audio visit:
www.halleonard.com/mylibrary

Enter Code
7212-7784-6132-0027

Audio Arrangements by Peter Deneff

ISBN 978-1-4950-2794-9

HAL•LEONARD®
CORPORATION
7777 W. BLUEMOUND RD. P.O. BOX 13819 MILWAUKEE, WI 53213

Visit Hal Leonard Online at
www.halleonard.com

ALL OF ME

Words and Music by JOHN STEPHENS
and TOBY GAD

NIGHT CHANGES

Words and Music by LOUIS TOMLINSON,
LIAM PAYNE, NIALL HORAN,
ZAYN MALIK, HARRY STYLES,
JULIAN BUNETTA, JAMIE SCOTT
and JOHN RYAN

Lyrics:

Go - ing out to - night; chang - es in - to some - thing red. Her moth - er does - n't like that kind of dress. Ev - 'ry - thing she nev - er had, she's show - ing off.

Chas - ing it to - night; doubts are run - nin' 'round her head. He's wait - ing; hides be - hind a cig - a - rette. Heart is beat - in' loud, and she does - n't want it to stop.

Go - ing out to - night; chang — es in - to some-thing red.

Her moth - er does — n't like that kind of dress; re -

minds her of the miss - ing piece ___ of in - no - cence she lost. ___

SAY SOMETHING

Words and Music by IAN AXEL,
CHAD VACCARINO and MIKE CAMPBELL

Say some-thing, I'm giv-ing up on you.

STAY WITH ME

Words and Music by SAM SMITH,
JAMES NAPIER and WILLIAM EDWARD PHILLIPS

Moderate Soul

Guess it's true, I'm not good at a one-night stand.
Why am I so e-mo-tion-al?

But I still need love 'cause I'm just a man.
No, it's not a good look. Gain some self-con-trol.

These nights nev-er seem to go to plan.
And deep down I know this nev-er works.

STYLE

Words and Music by TAYLOR SWIFT,
MAX MARTIN, SHELLBACK and ALI PAYAMI

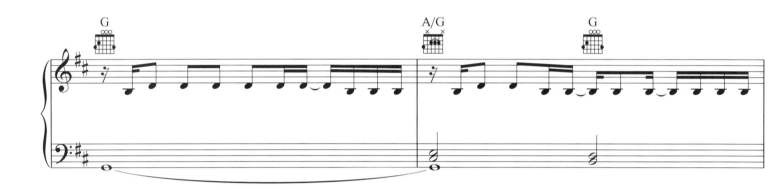

TAKE ME TO CHURCH

Words and Music by
ANDREW HOZIER-BYRNE

Moderate Ballad

My lov-er's got hu-mour, she's the gig-gle at a fu-n'ral.

Knows ev-'ry-bod-y's dis-ap-prov- al, I should've wor-shipped her soon-er.

If the heav-ens ev-er did speak, she's the last __ true mouth-piece. Ev-'ry Sun-day's get-ting more bleak,

THINKING OUT LOUD

Words and Music by ED SHEERAN
and AMY WADGE

will   be lov-ing you   till ___ we're se - ven - ty. ___   And ba - by, my
soul   could nev - er grow   old, ___ it's ev - er - green. _   And ba - by, your

heart   could still feel as   hard ___ at twen - ty - three. ___
smile's   for - ev - er in   my mind _ and mem - o - ry. ___

And I'm think-ing 'bout   how ___   Peo-ple fall in love in mys-ter - i-ous ways, ___
And I'm think-ing 'bout   how ___   peo-ple fall in love in mys-ter - i-ous ways, ___   and

UPTOWN FUNK

Words and Music by MARK RONSON,
BRUNO MARS, PHILIP LAWRENCE,
JEFF BHASKER, DEVON GALLASPY
and NICHOLAUS WILLIAMS

Upbeat Funk

This sh*t,_ that ice cold,_ Mi-

chelle Pfeif - fer, that white gold._ This one_ for them hood girls,_ them

Don't be - lieve _ me? Just watch.   Come on.

Don't be - lieve _ me? Just watch.

Don't be - lieve _ me? Just watch.

THE ULTIMATE SONGBOOKS

HAL·LEONARD
PIANO PLAY-ALONG

These great songbook/CD packs come with our standard arrangements for piano and voice with guitar chord frames plus a CD.

The CD includes a full performance of each song, as well as a second track without the piano part so you can play "lead" with the band! Volumes 86 and beyond also include the Amazing Slow Downer technology so PC and Mac users can adjust the recording to any tempo without changing the pitch!

HAL·LEONARD®
CORPORATION
7777 W. BLUEMOUND RD. P.O. Box 13819
MILWAUKEE, WISCONSIN 53213

Visit Hal Leonard Online at
www.halleonard.com

Prices, contents and availability subject to change without notice.
Disney characters and artwork © Disney Enterprises, Inc.

0